FR. THEOBALD MATHEW *OFM Cap*

The Apostle of Temperance

MOIRA LYSAGHT

GW00384735

FOUR COURTS PRESS

This book was typeset in 11 on 12pt IBM Baskerville
by Vermilion, Clondalkin, Co. Dublin for Four
Courts Press Limited, Kill Lane, Blackrock, Co.
Dublin.

© Moira Lysaght 1983

ISBN 0 906127 77 7

Printed by A. Wheaton & Co., Ltd., Exeter

CONTENTS

SOURCES

BOOKS

Augustine OFM Cap., Fr: *Footprints of Fr Theobald Mathew OFM Cap*, Dublin 1947

De Breffny, Brian: *Castles of Ireland*, London 1977

Burke's Irish Family Records, London 1974

Hayes, W.J.: *Holy Cross Abbey*

Lodge, John: *The Peerage of Ireland*, 4 vols, London 1974

Percy, Reuben and Sholto: *The Percy Anecdotes*, London n.d. (c. 1872)

Rogers, Patrick: *Father Theobald Mathew*, Dublin 1943

ARTICLES

Collins SJ, Fr Desmond: 'St Francis Xavier Church, Gardiner St 1832-1982': special issue of the *Irish Jesuit*, May 1982

Jones, Mark Bence: article on Thomastown Castle, *Country Life*, 2 October 1969

'An Irishman's Diary', *Irish Times*, 24 July 1980

Went, Arthur E.J.: 'Medallic Illustrations of Dublin History', *Dublin Historical Record*, June 1978.

INTRODUCTION

Although Co. Tipperary can justly claim Theobald Mathew as the most illustrious of her sons, to quote from the *Cork Constitution's* tribute after his death, 'Mr Mathew's reputation was not Irish nor English but European and American' — a comment which also indicated Protestants' high opinion of him.

In song and in story the names and deed of long-dead warrior-heroes have been passed down to us in detail while those who fought far greater moral battles are forgotten. How many people in the south of Ireland, on passing by 'The Statue' in Cork, regard it as only a meeting place or a point of direction and have no knowledge of the person whom it represents beyond a vague idea that 'he had something to do with temperance!' In Dublin no doubt there are many citizens who are not even aware of his statue in O'Connell St opposite the Gresham Hotel, nor could they answer a question as to his achievements.

It might seem strange to dwell on the statues of a man before going into the story of his life, and yet it does help to build up a mental picture and interest. In Cork the skilful work of Foley was unveiled in the presence of '100,000 persons gathered from every corner in Ireland' in 1864, after the friar's death. There it stands facing the visitor to Patrick St, dressed in the secular style of the day, whereas the Dublin statue, by Mary Redmond, portrayed him in the religious habit of a Franciscan Capuchin friar, to which order he belonged. It is the only such representation which I have come across, as at that period the wearing of the religious habit in public was not allowed by law.

A pen-picture of the priest's general appearance has been left to us by Kohl, the noted German traveller: 'His features are regular and full of a noble expression of mildness and indomitable firmness. He has a fine and delicate hand and dresses well, almost elegantly.'

THE HISTORY OF THE MATHEWS

The Mathew family is of Welsh origin and claims descent

from Sir David Mathew of Llandaff in Wales, standard-bearer to Edward IV. In 1485 William Mathew, David's grand-son, was made Knight Bannaret on Boswell Field by Henry Tudor, and from him descended the founder of the Irish branch, Captain George Mathew, eldest son of Edmond Mathew of Radyr, High Sheriff of Glamorgan in 1592. This George married Elizabeth, daughter of Sir John Pointz of Iron Acton in Gloucestershire, the widow of Thomas Butler, Viscount Thurles, who had been drowned off the Skerries in 1619.

Captain George came to Ireland about 1620 when he settled in Thurles on his wife's jointure lands which had for years been the property of the Butlers. He only occasionally returned to his Welsh property. Lady Thurles, although a Catholic, lived undisturbed in her castle at Thurles through-out the Cromwellian campaign, helping the oppressed Catholics of Tipperary, and was never without a chaplain in her home. She was acknowledged as the benefactress of the Archdiocese of Cashel. Her devotion to the Catholic faith was so well-known that her eldest son by her first marriage — James Butler — had been taken from her charge by the Royal warrant of James I and made a ward of the Archbishop of Canterbury 'who took care to have him instructed in the Protestant religion as professed in the Church of England', to quote John Lodge's *The Peerage in Ireland.*

Apart from James, Viscountess Thurles' five sons and five daughters from her two marriages were all deeply faithful to the Catholic religion and the Stuart cause. When death came to Lady Thurles in 1673 her instructions were carried out that her body 'be layed and buryed in the little Chapple called Our Ladyes Chapple near the parish Church in Thurles.'

Of her marriage to Captain George Mathew of Radyr there were three children — two boys, Theobald and George, and the girl Frances (who became a nun, lived on the continent and is buried in Thurles). From the two sons respectively there stemmed the Thurles-Annefield line of Mathews and the Thomastown branch in the same county of Tipperary. Theobald, the elder, was given the castle and dower lands of Thurles by his half-brother James who after the Restoration of the Stuarts in 1660 became first duke of Ormond and later was appointed Viceroy of Ireland by Charles II. George received the lands of Thomastown — near Cashel — from the same source (this latter estate had been the property of the

Augustinian Abbey of Athassel in Co. Tipperary until 13 September 1558 when it was granted to Thomas, Earl of Ormond by Mary Tudor. 'On the same day she confirmed that Holy Cross Abbey was also to pass to the Earl, as it did under Elizabeth in 1563'). In 1670 George Mathew had a two-storey house built on the land which, in the classical fashion set by his halfbrother's wife, the Duchess of Ormond, was of pink brick, like her mansion in Dunmore, Kilkenny.

Although the two lines of the Mathews were well disposed towards one another they were quite distinct in life-style. The Thomastown families were home-based and augmented their income by marrying into wealthy 'settlers' families'. The Thurles branch followed an Anglicised-Catholic-Jacobite line and their wealth was increased by the Welsh property which descended to them as senior representatives of the Mathews. Theobald, the founder of this branch, had married as his third wife Catherine Neville of Leicestershire, and a daughter of this marriage became a maid of honour at the Court of Saint Germaine to Queen Mary, consort of James II, while a son became a Jesuit.

The first member of either branch to conform to the Established Church was Lady Thurles' great-grandson, George of Thomastown, who became known as Grand George. In 1711 he had inherited the estate with its large undecorative mansion, but due to penal laws of the time he was unable to enter fully into such social life as his extravagant nature desired. This would appear to be the more likely reason for his change of religion than that he feared the forfeiture of his estate through enactment of the same laws, as stated in one biography.

In order to satisfy his ambition to devote his life to the lavish entertainment of others, this George retired to the continent for seven years, living there thriftily until he had saved up almost £70,000 from his annual income of £10,000. He then returned home and had extensive internal and external renovations carried out on the house and grounds. These included fifty extra bedrooms; the purchase of twenty finest hunters; packs of hounds; an outdoor theatre; bowling greens; landscaped ponds and terraces, with many other sidelines. Abstemious himself, he satisfied any alcholic desire of his guests for the round of the clock, but in a secluded part of the house. Meals were supplied in accordance with the taste of each guest — in their rooms or in the dining hall as desired, no specified meal-time observance needing to be adhered to. 'No tipping' was a strict rule and instant dismissal awaited an infringement by a servant. The large staff was liberally paid to avoid this evil.

Dean Swift, influenced by his friend Dr Sheridan, accepted an invitation to Thomastown (although no invitation was necessary); Dr Sheridan was a frequent visitor, being tutor to a nephew of George's. At an intervening hostelry, which they reached on horseback and where they intended to stay the night, they found awaiting them a coach and six horses which had been dispatched by their prospective host to take them the rest of their journey. With it were choicest wines and foods for their refreshment en route.

Coming in sight of the mansion the Dean cried out 'What in the name of God can be the use of such a vast building?' Hearing that it contained fifty guestrooms, which were always occupied, it was with difficulty that Sheridan persuaded his companion to continue the journey — the Dean complaining as he went 'I must submit but I have lost a fortnight of my life.' They were greeted at the entrance by Grand George who, having shown the Dean to his room, delivered his usual speech to newly-arrived guests: 'This is your castle; here you are to command absolutely, as in your own house. You may breakfast, dine and sup here whenever you please; from this on you are never to know me as master of the house but only to consider me as one of the guests.' (As proof of the sincerity of this latter intention the host used to take his place at table at random.)

After spending three days riding and wandering around the estate, avoiding in general what he presumed would be 'a motley crowd', the Dean finally entered the room where the company was assembled for dinner. There he bestowed lavish praise on the host for his artistic skill and taste of connoisseur as shown in his general layout of the estate. Subsequently he entered into all the entertainments and his planned two weeks' visit extended to four months.

Grand George married twice; by his first wife Elizabeth Butler of Ballyragget, Co. Kilkenny, he had one son; but he predeceased him. On Elizabeth's death he married Anne, widow of James de la Poer, Earl of Tyrone. When he died in 1737-8 he was succeeded by his grandson George, a child of five years. The guardian of this child was his uncle and first cousin-once-removed, another George, the head of the

Thurles family. The close double relationship (of uncle plus first-cousin once-removed) between the child and George is accounted for by the fact that the child's mother, Mary Anne Mathew, was a sister of George of Thurles Castle and she had married her first cousin Theobald of Thomastown, son of Grand George. On Theobald's early death she had married an O'Hara of Kinsealy, Co. Dublin.

In the same year of his succession this child drowned in the lake. Locally, it was held that his guardian had arranged the drowning and that his death brought down his mother's curse, predicting that never would the Thomastown estate pass from father to son and that the Mathew family would cease to exist in Tipperary. (Although, to quote the words of Archbishop Mathew, 'This story seems to have been entirely without foundation', yet subsequent events caused it to be a subject of conjecture, for the sons of George the guardian, from his two marriages, predeceased him, leaving only a daughter; and, in time to come, the last male Mathew occupants of Thomastown, the three sons of the first earl of Llandaff, died without issue).

George of Thurles, the guardian, now became the inheritor of Thomastown, and the Thurles line took over the conjoined estates to which were added the estates of Radyr and Llandaff which had descended to the Thurles family as senior members of the Mathews. From 1740 onwards George of Thurles was known as George of Thomastown. When he died, in 1760, it was found he had willed the combined estates to a cousin, Thomas Mathew of Annefield, near Thurles. The will was unsuccessfully disputed by George's only daughter, Margaret, wife of Michael Aylmer of Lyons, Co. Kildare. Thomas, like George, was a Catholic, but later, due to the fact he was disqualified from becoming a member at the parliamentary election in 1761, he and his son Francis conformed to the Established Church in the same year.

Francis, the next holder of the conjoined properties, now a member of parliament for Co. Tipperary, was in 1783 raised to the peerage of Ireland as Baron Llandaff, which title he took from the seat of his Welsh ancestors. Later he gained a viscountcy and in 1797 an earldom. He voted against the Union and he founded a regiment of Volunteers in Tipperary. In 1806 he died. It is stated that neither he nor his children ever attended a Protestant church. They were married in the drawingroom of their family house in Merrion Square,

Dublin; as were their close connections, the Talbots of Malahide.

Francis, the first earl of Llandaff, was twice married; his first wife was Elizabeth ('Ellis') Smyth of Tinna Park, Co. Wicklow, a wealthy heiress; after her death he married Lady Catherine Skeffington, daughter of the first earl of Massereene.

That duelling was used by members of the Mathew family in the settlement of disputes is shown in the following quotation 'Lord Viscount Llandaff (which probably was the second earl, Francis James, generally entitled 'Viscount') fought a duel with Lord Clonmel'.

Another article in an old newspaper gave an account of outstanding skill in this form of combat by a 'John' Mathew — which name in that generation I have not come across elsewhere in my research: 'John Mathew having inherited his father's wealth, spent a seven years' visit in Paris and on his return he spent two months in his home in Dorset Street, Dublin, where he gave great parties. Duelling was his big thing, word of which reached two army gentlemen, noted duellists in England, and they came over to Dublin to challenge him. When he was pointed out to them as he passed in a sedan chair they jostled against it, throwing him out but he took it to be an accident and passed on. Later in a bar the Major Pratt and Captain Creed declared openly that Mathew had refused to fight. James MacNamara, a friend of the latter having being present, went to Dorset Street after which both himself and Mathew — sword in hand — went to the inn. In the subsequent duel both Englishmen were wounded but recovered later.' In view of the similarity of time spent in France and the propensity for giving large parties, could it not have been Grand George and not so-called 'John' who featured here?

To return to Francis: a big drain was put on the estate by his entanglement in politics, by his wife Elizabeth's patronage of fashion, and by their extensive travels abroad, which included even visits to the French Court. A valuable painting of Elizabeth — 'Mrs Mathew Portrait' — by Joshua Reynolds is in Capetown. When she died in 1781 there were '150 mourning coaches and 120 domestics dressed in black' at the funeral.

Francis had three sons: Francis James, 2nd earl of Llandaff; Major General Montagu; and George; also a daughter, Lady Elizabeth. The sons were friends of the Prince Regent until a quarrel arose when they changed their support to Queen Caroline. They were popular landlords, enemies of the Administration and opponents of the Act of Union like their father. They held all the Tipperary seats in Parliament. The three of them were portrayed as 'The Three Mr Wigans' by Gillray.

The wealth of the estate dwindled further with their extravagant gambling and general high living. Francis James, the second earl and inheritor of the estate, being influenced by a wave of castle-building, decided to change their simple, classical-styled home into a Tudor castle, engaging for the purpose Richard Morrison, a well-known architect. The former pink-brick exterior was covered over and bedecked with battlements and turrets. Gothic tracery flowed over the inner walls. Outside, a triumphal arch was constructed, but money ran out before a designed Roman tower was added. To meet his losses he sold Thurles Castle and the Welsh property.

Like his forefathers the second earl was a good landlord. His brother Major-General Montagu (who never · lost an opportunity in Parliament to urge the claims of the Catholics) was one of the last 'Four Bottle Men' in the county. He died in 1819 at dinner in Castle Fogarty. None of the three brothers left issue and so the earldom became extinct.

Their sister, Lady Elizabeth — the next inheritor — had not married and at her death in 1841 she left the estate away from the Mathew family, to a first cousin on her mother's side — Viscount Rohan de Chabot, who visited Thomastown each summer with his son, Comte de Jarnac, and gave large house parties until the latter's death in 1872, after which the property went to Lord Dunsandle who lived in Galway and rarely visited it.

The house gradually fell into ruin, being deserted by the caretakers in the 'troubled times' around 1921, and eventually large portions of the masonry were carted away by local farmers for their own use. In 1938, Archbishop David Mathew, a great-grand nephew of Fr Theobald, bought the ivy-covered ruin and twenty surrounding acres, for sentimental reasons. The following year a white marble figure of the friar, surrounded by an iron railing on a limestone kerb was erected outside the entrance to the Castle. Beneath Fr Theobald's name is inscribed 'Unveiled 25 June 1939 by

David Mathew, Auxiliary Bishop of Westminster, the great-grandson of his brother. It was erected at his birthplace by the Pioneer Association and other friends in Tipperary and the adjoining counties.'

Deliberating on the unauthenticated curse, the fact of the lack of direct heirs to the property and the final extinction of the castle and the Mathew name therein raise a question in one's mind: could not the cause of the fall of the family be taken as an act of retribution for the forfeiture and destruction (in 1558) of the ancient Augustinian Abbey of Athassel and its monks? Archbishop Mathew stated in an article on the family that 'when Fr Mathew died in 1856 there were no more Mathews in Co. Tipperary.'

To provide some details of the subsequent fortunes of the family as given by *Country Life* and *Irish Sketch and Tatler*: 'Fr Mathew's nephews and their descendants left Co. Tipperary for England where they received remarkable distinction in many walks of life. His grand-niece Elizabeth, the daughter of the Lord Justice Mathew, returned to Ireland as the wife of the Nationalist leader — John Dillon.' Their son James, a noted orator, was Minister of Agriculture and leader of the Fine Gael party. 'In more recent years the family had included the late Sir Theobald Mathew, Director of Public Prosecutions; the late Mr Francis Mathew, manager of *The Times*, as well as Archbishop David Mathew and his brother Fr Gervase Mathew, both eminent scholars and writers.'

I have not come across written accounts of other descendants of the large family of twelve to which Fr Mathew himself belonged. Personal knowledge, however, fills in a gap regarding one, the Temperance Advocate's sister Kate, who married Michael Lysaght of Lisowen, Co. Limerick, and both of whom thereby in time became my great-grandparents; Fr Theobald, therefore, was my great-granduncle. Their son was called Charles, which was the name of the Friar's favourite brother and has remained in our family ever since (it had descended to the Mathews from the Shelley family).

FR MATHEW'S IMMEDIATE FAMILY

Now to place Fr Theobald in the jig-saw picture of the Mathew family. With the ending of the Thomastown line when

George of Thurles Castle became the uniter of the two Tipperary estates which later he bequeated to his cousin Thomas of Annefield, it fell to the Thurles Mathews to perpetuate the family through that Thomas and his uncle James of Two-Mile-Borris, near Thurles. The latter was a great-grandson of George of Radyr and was a grandfather of Fr Theobald as the latter himself stated. That branch had remained Catholic. The biographer of Fr Mathew, Patrick Rogers, states that 'James of Borris's father had fought at Aughrim and had links with the Wild Geese. Another item of interest is the fact that a niece of James's was Nano Nagle, foundress of the Presentation order.'

Archbishop Mathew in an account of the family lineage stated that he had evidence to show that 'James the orphan' (Fr Theobald's father) was the son of a second marriage between James of Borris with Anne O'Rahill, who died in childbirth. There were also two girls by either that second marriage or by James's first wife, Anne Morres of Borris. Of these girls, Anne, the elder, became Mrs Francis Kearney and the other became Mrs John Hunt; the husbands of both were members of the local Protestant gentry.

After the joining of the properties the family interest was now focussed on Thomastown with its long bare mansion. James the orphan had been taken from Thurles at an early age by his cousin Francis, first earl of Llandaff and head of the house, to live at Thomastown with himself and his unmarried daughter, Lady Elizabeth. When James reached manhood he was made agent of the property and not long afterwards he married his first cousin Anne Whyte, the daughter of Squire George Whyte of Cappawhite and his wife Mary, who was a younger daughter of Theobald of Thomastown and his wife Mary Anne (formerly of Thurles). They lived on in the Castle.

THE YOUNG TOBY MATHEW

Of this union there were nine boys and three girls. The fourth son, Theobald, the future Temperance Advocate, was born on 10 October 1790. For the first five years of his life, Toby, as his family called him, enjoyed the grandeur of his surroundings within the mansion and throughout the two-thousand acre demesne with its spacious, well laid out gardens, woods, and droves of red deer. By that time, however, the earl, bewildered by the rapid increase in additions to his agent's family, had a large residence built for them at Rathclogheen, on the estate. Naturally the children must have found the change disappointing but they were free and welcome to visit the castle and to roam around the grounds at will.

At an early age Toby displayed the characteristics which later were to influence people and achieve the success of his mission. Cheerful in manner, helpful to all in distress, especially the poor in the surrounding district, who called him 'Darlin' Master Toby, a born saint', the name of God was held by him in the highest reverence.

The giving of treats to his companions caused him great pleasure but he would not join in their boisterous amusements. His gentle nature and love of animals caused him to refuse to accompany his brothers and their friends on their coursing and ferreting expeditions: this reserve brought down on him rough criticism. He took pleasure in quiet walks alone or with one or two friends. Later, with the development of manhood, Dr Owen Madden, a contemporary of his, attributed these distinguishing features to his ancestry and background: 'To great suavity of manners, which was a prominent characteristic of his deportment, he joined dignity of carriage and a composed serenity of mind. A steady self-control presided over all his acts and emotions. A cordial politeness and unvarying affability distinguished him.' In 1798 he was only eight years old when tales filtered through from the neighbouring counties of the cruel treatment doled out by the dreaded yeomen to the defeated rebels — the pitch-capping, floggings, hangings, triangle tortures, burning of homesteads and such. All of this influenced his later missionary appeal to the people to refrain from any connection with secret societies and also his strongly voiced disapproval of revolutionary organisations. In years to come his fight against the demon of intemperance — that even greater tyrannical conqueror of his country — was to be carried out and won without the shedding of a single drop of blood.

To return to his childhood and its religious surroundings: naturally an attitude towards the Catholic faith would not have been a foremost subject of conversation at the castle, and it has been surmised that Toby's father — James the agent's — adherence to his religious duties was not of a marked character. The latter's wife, however, carried on the Mathew tradition, on her mother's side, of fervent adherence to the Old Faith. She had a great desire that at least one of her sons would become a priest, and it seemed this would be fulfilled in her son George, until one day he declared to the assembled family that he had changed his mind. The disappointed mother declared, 'Is it not unfortunate, I have nine sons and not one of them to be a priest!' The strained silence which followed was broken by the clear voice of Toby: 'Mother, don't be uneasy, I will be a priest.'

Although none of the Mathew family had up to that entered the priesthood, their close blood and marriage connections — the Butlers — had produced three successive archbishops of Cashel and at the time of Toby's birth, the third of these — James Butler — held that position. Toby's open declaration of intention to be a priest had a marked effect on his brothers and increased his influence over them, an influence which grew stronger down the years. His soft and gentle voice and manner used to calm the hasty, independent traits of his favourite brother, Charles, just as in time he disarmed the would-be opponents in his campaign.

Toby's early education took place in the Market House in Thurles, at a school run by a Mr Flynn and where he became a friend of a fellow pupil — Charles Bianconi — who was later to become famous as the pioneer of stage-coaching in Ireland. That friendship started when Bianconi received a blow on the nose from a belligerent companion and Toby rushed to the rescue, stopping the resultant flow of blood.

Young Toby's tuition was later put into the hands of a Fr Denis O'Donnell until he was ten years old, when he was sent as a boarder to St Canice's 'The Old Academy', Kilkenny, at the wish and personal expense of his cousin, Lady Elizabeth, who was very well disposed to all the young family, but above all to Toby, her god-son. St Canice's, a very highly thought-of educational academy, was situated on part of the site of the present Loreto Convent.

After seven years in Kilkenny, during which time he received prizes in Greek, Latin and English history, more through diligent study than brilliance, he applied at the age of seventeen years for entrance to Maynooth College where he matriculated in September 1807. In the Matriculation Book dated 6 April 1808 his signature — 'Tobias Mathew' — showed how he still used the family form of his first name.

It is not known how long he spent in Maynooth but it was evidently sufficient to gain him new friendships. His desire in that direction prompted him to risk the breaking of rules by inviting some companions to his room to an informal party — à la Grand George — even if infinitesimal in comparison. The entrance of a dean, who had heard sounds of merriment, resulted in the suspension of the culprit while his case was being considered. Knowing that the order of expulsion was inevitable, the rule being regarded as very strict, Toby did not wait but left quietly one morning.

Several months were spent at home where the kindness of his mother and all the family compounded his sorrow. Added to this was the shame that he had let down Fr McGrath of St Canice's, who had so highly recommended him, and also the knowledge that he could not apply to the archbishop for entrance to another ecclesiastical college.

His one hope of guidance now rested in prayer, in which his mother fervently joined. The answer came in his remembrance of two old Capuchin friars whom he used to see and possibly with whom he had spoken during his schooldays in Kilkenny. Their general demeanour on the streets, and the fervour with which they prayed in their little shabby chapel, came to his mind and led him onwards. An application to join the order received a consent from the Provincial, Father John Baptist Leonard, and changed the sorrowing heart to one of joy. The journey through the Valley of Darkness had strengthened his character; had taught him the seriousness of life; the realization of the power of prayer and had led him into the Franciscan-Capuchin Order; a congregation where his good qualities of selflessness, dedication to the poor and deference to authority would have full scope; the Capuchins at the time were quoted as being 'the poorest and weakest of the religious fraternities in Ireland.' The momentous event took place early in 1810. On 4 February in that year Theobald was received as a novice in the little friary near Church St, Dublin and, as was then, and still is, customary in that order, he took a saint's name, in his case Andrew, but he always signed himself Theobald Mathew as the Government's strict regulations against religious order had not yet been officially revoked.

To give a short history of the Capuchin order: it was

started in Italy in 1523 with a down-to-earth object of close contact being kept with all classes and under all circumstances, poverty having a high priority in their charitable efforts. The friars' heroism during the wave of pestilence which swept through mid-Europe in their formative days established their success as missionaries.

Their introduction to Ireland was due to an Irishman, Francis Nugent, son of Sir Thomas Nugent of Moyrath Castle, Co. Meath. Having been educated in Paris and Louvain (scholarship being banned in his own country), he became a Capuchin friar in 1591 in Brussels and had risen high in the order. There were only five members in the first batch which arrived in Dublin in 1615 and they lived separately in private houses until Fr Francis made his first visitation in 1624 and acquired a house in Bridge St, where the friars started to live in community until a change was made to North King St; not long later, in 1720, a move was made to nearby Church St, their present abode.

Long before Theobald joined as a novice, most of the foundations throughout the country had been shut down owing to persecution, and vocations had become rare, but a rise in the tide of recovery was evident. The little chapel first erected in Church St was enlarged and rebuilt about 1796 and there the young Tipperary aspirant witnessed daily the deep devotion of the poverty-stricken people. In more recent times we may visualise the figure of the sixteen-year-old James Joyce stumbling grief-stricken into a Church St confessional box.

Having completed his noviceship of preparation, Theobald was ordained on Holy Saturday, 17 April 1813, in St Andrew's Church, Townsend St on the site of which there stood a convent of the Sisters of Mercy up to a few years ago when their school was transferred nearby. A plaque on the wall of the deserted building gives details of the Ordination.

Dr Daniel Murray, Coadjutor Archbishop of Dublin, who performed the ceremony, was himself to leave behind him an outstanding record of ecclesiastical achievement as evidenced by the ninety-seven large prominently-placed new churches which he built in his dioceses in contrast to the earlier hidden away places of worship in transformed stables, storehouses and such, with the exception of Clarendon St and St Michael and John's. Added to this he was responsible for the formation of the Irish Sisters of Charity, to be followed by the Loreto Order and later the Sisters of Mercy. In years to come Archbishop Murray was the first to hail Fr Mathew as 'The Apostle of Temperance.'

A CAPUCHIN IN KILKENNY

After his ordination Fr Theobald paid what must have been to him a very sad visit to his old home, Rathclogheen, as both his parents had died during his novitiate. At his celebration of Mass in Kilfeacle, a neighbouring parish, at the request of the parish priest he delivered a sermon on his favourite subject, poverty. As Lady Elizabeth, his god-mother, was then in residence at Thomastown Castle, only two miles distant, she may have been present at his sermon and a presentation of a chalice which was made to him while at home was probably a gift from her. He prized it greatly and later had engraved around the base the words 'Pray for the souls of James and Anne Mathew, of Thomastown.'

Shortly after the young priest's return to Church St he was transferred to the friary in Kilkenny where his arrival made up a community of three — himself and the two elderly priests whom, as a young student, he had so admired. They were dependent for sustenance on the offerings of the people, whose poor circumstances were further hampered by the obligation of contributing to the Established Church and also to their own parish clergy — all of which left very little over for the friars. The friary was an old hay loft in what is now Friars St. It was said that they 'brewed their own ale and baked their own bread.'

The new arrival, with his youthful, earnest dedication, his gentle winning way and zeal for souls, gradually filled their 'Poor House Chapel' from where his fame as a kindly, understanding confessor spread. In less than a year however, all this came to an abrupt end with a most tragic happening in the life of the young cleric. The circumstances connected with this would be so incomprehensible at the present that an explanation seems necessary. During the Penal Law period the mendicant orders had kept the faith alive among the people, to whom the Franciscan friars living in hiding had preached the duty of loyalty to the Vicar of Christ, against the attempt to enforce the doctrine of Royal Supremacy in religion. The friars' influence with the people, which continued after the enactments fell into abeyance, aroused uneasiness among the diocesan clergy, who regarded their source of revenue as being depleted by the people's contribution to the religious Orders. Requests to the bishops to remedy this resulted in several regulations, one of which forbade the faithful from receiving Easter Communion in Order chapels.

At the time of this unfortunate incident the bishop of the diocese having died, the vicar capitular in temporary charge had been wrongly informed that Fr Mathew had administered Easter Communion in the Capuchin chapel. Without enquiring further he had sent a clergyman with a letter direct to the friar in his confessional. Having read the note Fr Theobald stood up and, addressing the large Saturday crowd of penitents said, 'Go to your other clergymen. I have no power to hear your confessions any longer'; after which he left the chapel. Rumours spread through the city, many of which were that the priest had been suspended for some misdeed. In a few days, however, the true account of the accusation and the falsity of the allegation was made known. The vicar capitular offered sincere apologies and the restoration of the faculties for confession. Feeling that he would have lost the confidence of the people, Fr Mathew's superiors, to spare him further embarrassment, changed him to Cork, where his missionary field flourished from 1814 to 1838.

HIS MISSION IN CORK

Here, with Fr Daniel Francis Donovan, the superior in charge of the friary, the new arrival made up a community of two in the obscurity of Blackamoor Lane at the back of Sullivan's Quay, the quarters of the most poverty-stricken, whose houses were more like dens.

On the day of his arrival, the superior, having welcomed him and having shown him around the city, took him to be introduced to friends, where he left him with instructions to await his return. As time passed and he did not come, the sensitive young friar's embarrassment rocketed when dinner was announced. Hurriedly he rose to go but was prevailed on to stay. Later he came to realize that the brusque but kindhearted Fr Donovan (who was known to have literally 'given the shirt of his back' to a poor man) had thought out that ruse because the friary cupboard had not the wherewithal to provide a decent meal for a traveller. The bed-clothes for his room had been borrowed.

To quote an account of the friary chapel as given later, in 1868: it was 'remarkable for its dwarfish dimensions, its utter want of architectual grace and its perfect seclusion from the public gaze when it was built, lest its presence should awaken official conscience to enforce penal law legislation'. It was only 30 feet long by 43 feet wide. Two side-galleries had been built but they were so close together that it was said that a person in one could almost shake hands with someone opposite.

The living quarters of the two friars consisted of two small rooms and a kind of closet adjoining the back gallery, which later held a little organ and chair. As the community increased in time a change was made to a house in Cove St, which was connected to the sacristy by a passageway. Later, when Fr Theobald's abstinence crusade progressed and hundreds of people came seeking him, a further removal was made to a larger house, No. 10 Cove St.

For the next twenty-four years, until his Total Abstinence mission commenced, Fr Mathew devoted all his time and energy to the poor people surrounding Blackamoor Lane, as he had done in Kilkenny. Soon his reputation as a confessor spread, due to his sympathetic approach to penitents, and frequently he was found seated in his confessional box as early as five in the morning to facilitate night- and early-morning workers. Also to accomodate those not versed in English he learned Irish to a tolerably good speaking level.

With the present-day vast improvement in wealth and consequently hygiene, it would be difficult to realize the atmospheric conditions which then prevailed in Blackamoor Lane Chapel, enough to overwhelm with revulsion the sensitive, refined confessor in his 'wardrobe'-like enclosure, as a confession-box has recently been aptly referred to by Fr Michael Cleary. It took a great deal of time and endurance before the abnoxious smell of unwashed bodies and clothing of the poor and the stench from workers in chandlery, butchers from slaughter houses, fish vendors and such in the cooped-up enclosure, became tolerable to the young friar who became known to rich and poor as 'the sinner's friend'.

One Sunday morning, having spent four hours in the 'box' before he had celebrated Mass and again following it, as he left the chapel for breakfast four sailors approached him for confession. Being tired out, rebellious nature prompted him to reprimand them for not being there at the regular time and tell them to come back next morning. As they were going away an old woman standing nearby addressed him saying, 'They may not come again, Sir' and hurriedly the priest followed them and brought them back and having confessed them he invited them to join him at breakfast.

His fame as a confessor attracted many to hear him preach, and wealthy parishioners from other city and surrounding country parishes took their place among the poor in the little chapel.He was not a gifted orator nor did he possess a powerful voice; actually a critic referred to it as weak but later the same critic said, 'At his affectionate, earnest and pathetic exhortation, all that was in us unkind and harsh, was softened down; our hearts beat only to kindlier emotions; we sympathised with our fellow Christians around us.' In later years, through practice, his voice had strengthened by the time he had to address thousands at meetings.

In his main objective of help for the poor he started a school for girls in a converted store near the chapel, where girls were taught simple school subjects and also were instructed in housework and sewing. In 1824 there were 500 pupils, which included grown girls, and the instruction was carried out by charitably disposed ladies. For the boys he set up a night school where the instructors were young men members of the Josephian Society, which he founded in 1819; it was an organisation similar to our St Vincent de Paul. In this selection of instructors Fr Theobald had a dual purpose in mind; it encouraged the better-off boys to help their less fortunate brothers, whom they also visited in their homes apart from school tuition.

Alms-giving was a great speciality with the friar: 'Give, give, have no fear of giving; what you have you got from God' was his dictum. Money as mass offerings or as gifts started to flow in, but it went out as quickly to the crowd of beggars at the friary door. To a friend who argued that this encouraged professional spongers, the priest replied. 'It is better to be deceived by nineteen imposters than to allow a deserving man to depart unrelieved.'

In 1824 Fr Theobald was inconsolable at the news of the death of his brother Robert, the youngest of the family, on a voyage with his brother Charles who was engaged in African trade. Robert had been left in the care of Fr Theobald and lived in the Friary while a student in Cork, but he had been attracted by the prospect of the sea journey.

The Provincial of the Capuchin order having died, Fr Mathew was elected to that high and exacting office in 1822 and held it for over twenty nine years, until failing health caused his resignation.

He was unhappy that because all the graveyards in Cork were under Protestant control, permission had to be obtained by priests in order to officiate at Catholic burials. This permission was frequently only grudgingly given and having personally witnessed an attempt by the Protestant Dean of Cork to prevent the Catholic Dean from officiating at an interment in St Finbarr's Churchyard, Fr Mathew's mind was made up to provide a burial ground of their own for Catholics. As a result of a well-supported subscription, the Botanic gardens were leased and opened in February 1830 and designated as St Joseph's Cemetery. A portion was set aside for free burial of the poor, whose bodies previous to that were left in their open coffins outside their dwellings until sufficient money was collected for their interment.

This achievement was to be followed two years later by the fulfilment of his ambition to provide a more fitting and extensive place of worship for his congregation. This was made possible by the passing of Catholic Emancipation some years before. On his birthday, 10 October 1832, the foundation stone was laid of the Capuchin Church of the Holy Trinity on Charlotte Quay — later named Fr Mathew Quay. The church was completed in 1850 at the cost of £10,000 and paid for by subscription, both Protestant and Catholic citizens donating £5,000 to which the friar added £4,500 from his own resources, a large portion of which came from his family. Dedicated to the Holy Trinity, it was opened for worship in October 1850. A stained glass window was inserted as a memorial to Daniel O'Connell, 'the Liberator'.

The long interval between the laying of the foundation stone and the completion of the church was due to many adverse factors, including building difficulties (marshland foundation having to be dealt with) and above all the tragic outbreak of Asiatic fever in the very foundation year of 1832. The cholera spread throughout the poor quarters of Cork and a large temporary hospital was opened in Blackamoor Lane near the Friary. The Capuchin community took it in turn to remain around the clock in the building as deaths occurred hourly. In the arrangement of duty Fr Mathew insisted that he be assigned the time from midnight until six in the morning. His outstanding courage and diligence won the admiration of all classes and creeds and his name became a by-word even in the years before the start of his special mission.

THE CORK TOTAL ABSTINENCE SOCIETY

That special campaign against the flagrant misuse of drink did not start with Fr Mathew nor in Ireland nor even in Europe but in America where temperance societies existed before the end of the eighteenth century. In 1817 the first total abstinence society in Ireland and possibly in Europe was formed by Jeffry Sedwards, a nailer in Skibbereen, Co. Cork, but it was merely local among artisans and tradespeople of that town.

A more impressive movement — claimed to have been the first Irish Temperance Society — against the use of spirits was founded in New Ross in 1829 by Rev. Whitmore Carr, Congregational Minister of that town of Wexford. The following month, the Ulster Temperance Society was established by Rev. Dr Edgar who was encouraged by Carr's action and was greatly impressed by the sermons of Rev. Ward Beecher (father of Harriet Beecher Stowe) on the evils of intemperance. These societies and their branches were, however, mostly confined to non-Catholics, and therefore had very little impact on the general evil of drunkenness. Three years later, in September 1832, a total abstinence campaign was launched in Lancashire, drunkenness being also widespread in England and Scotland.

A Dublin Total Abstinence Society was launched some years later, in 1836, and in October of that year a Great Temperance Banquet was held in the Rotunda, Dublin. There Judge Philip Cecil Crampton made an impressive speech in which he declared pledged moderation in drinking pattern to be ineffectual, arguing that total abstinence was the only course to lead to success.

Influenced by this speech several workers in the cause in Cork united their efforts. Prominent among these was a James McKenna, an ex-soldier; also Rev. Colthurst Dunscombe and William Martin, a member of the Society of

[23]

Friends. As the latter, an elderly Quaker, was holding a temperance meeting in an old theatre in Cook St., a crowd of anti-prohibitionists rushed in and, breaking up the furniture, showered abuse on what they called 'an insult to Irish hospitality in this imitation of English puritanical ways'. They succeeded in breaking up the meeting. More determined than ever, Quaker Martin held a further meeting at his house in Patrick St, which thirty people attended. A resolution was passed and a form of pledge drawn up by him starting with the words 'I promise to abstain from all intoxicating drink' was signed, first by him and then by the others present. Brave William Martin had started Total Abstinence in Cork but gradually members fell away; opposition and ridicule were showered on the head of the unappreciated Quaker, who was thought to have gone mad. Nothing daunted and supported by other active organisers, meeting places were opened throughout the city, one of which was in the Protestant school in Cove St, near the Capuchin Friary where Fr Mathew lived.

Realising that no great progress was being made, William Martin set his mind on recruiting the aid of Fr Mathew, whose cheerful, gentle manner, supported by a proven resolute mind and steadfast will, would rally the Catholics (who needed it most), among which body his name and reputation were a by-word. To set this plan in motion, a deputation from the Cove St branch called on the friar to solicit his aid but, although received kindly, they got no promise of help from him. Nothing daunted, Martin took another line of action. As both he and Fr Mathew were governors of the House of Industry (later the Cork Workhouse), Martin took advantage of each new tragic case of degradation which came before them to impress on the priest that it was the result of strong drink and how he could do so much against it. Providence lent a helping hand in an incident that occurred some time later. A statement which was made at a temperance meeting by a Protestant minister had offended the Catholic members, who left in a body. Seeking advice as to how they would act further, a prominent member met Fr Mathew by chance and, the latter having asked for information about the working of the Total Abstinence Movement, requested a meeting with the members at his Josephian Society venue. When that took place, Fr Mathew encouraged free discussion to which he listened attentively and then he promised to think things over and to give his decision in a month's time in the Schoolroom in Blackamoor Lane.

During the interval his mind wrestled with opposing thoughts: should he join forces in a movement which the majority of people considered to be a type of lunacy?; would it not be cowardly to refuse for a second time after having consented to meet the members?; would his joining cause a rift with the many good people with whom social custom entailed the provision of strong drink as a necessary accompanyment of entertainment at every social, political and religious meeting including christenings and marriages, funerals, American wakes and bargaining at fairs?; would his action cause offence with his fellow priests?; how could such a society succeed when so many, including the Bishop of Kildare and Leighlin, had failed — he who in 1834 had proclaimed in a pastoral that 'like the prophet he was hoarse with crying out against this appalling vice and yet it neither ceased or diminished'. From his own personal point of view, if the mission should prove successful, would it not bring ruin on his brother at Cashel and his brother-in-law at Midleton, both proprietors of distilleries? If he failed he knew that his influence, built up over the years, would be weakened, especially with the poor. Finally, when his mind was made up, his first resolution was not to ask the people to do what he had not done himself and so he would publicly renounce the personal taking of intoxicating drink, which in actual fact he had privately abstained from for some time.

Having spent a previous night in prayer, on the appointed evening addressing a large body of people attracted by news of his expected presence, he referred to having been influenced by the self-sacrifice of others, many of whom differed from him in religion. In a self-effacing speech declaring their misconception of his abilities and their unawareness of his defects, he continued: 'If through any humble instrumentality of mine, I can do good to my fellow creatures and give glory to God, I feel I am bound as a minister of the Gospel to throw all personal considerations aside and try to give a helping hand.' He ended by saying, 'I will be the first to sign my name in the book which is on the table and I hope we shall soon have it full.' Taking the pen in his hand and after a moment's pause (on that momentous Tuesday, 10 April 1838, the twenty-fifth of his ministry, and aged 48 years) he declared in a clear voice the famous words: 'Here goes in the Name of God', as he signed the register of the Cork Total Abstinence Society with 'Revd. Theobald Mathew, O.C., Cove Street, No. 1.'

Next day posters throughout the city announcing that Fr Mathew, President of the Cork Total Abstinence Society, would speak on the subject in his Schoolroom, Blackamoor Lane, were greeted by sneers and disbelief, yet the room was packed and a reported 330 members were enrolled at that second meeting. Very soon the number of people attending at the Schoolroom and seeking Fr Mathew at the friary increased so rapidly that new quarters had to be sought; eventually a venue was donated by Mrs O'Connor, the owner of the nearby Horse Bazaar on Sullivan's Quay, capable of holding 4,000 people. Criticism and opposition there was in plenty but the priest's standing with the poor, and the admiration of the rich of all creeds, carried weight, as did his argument that the objective of moderation had failed to overcome the abuse.

THE TEMPERANCE MOVEMENT SPREADS

Quickly word of his mission spread and crowds came from all over Munster and as far away as Galway. The small, though larger, house at No. 10 Cove St, to which the community had removed before he had joined the movement, became the mecca of an ever increasing crowd of pleading relatives and reluctant and frequently aggressive victims; as well as interested spectators, some from overseas. An acounnt from one such ran thus: 'We entered an apartment which, with the exception of a small one where he slept, was his only room and served him for meals, study and the reception of visitors. Not more than 16 ft. wide, its well-washed floor never knew the weight of the smallest carpet.'

One afternoon the neighbourhood was set agog by the sight of seven uniformed non-commissioned officers leading 300 men of the 45th Regiment of Foot to the door of the friary, where Fr Mathew, after giving them the pledge, presented each with a medal and card. This procedure of giving medals and cards free of charge was to place the unbusinesslike donor in serious trouble and possibly land him in jail. When he left Cork in December 1839 on his first temperance mission — at which time there were almost 10,000 names on the books — he was £1,500 in debt.

The enthusiasm which he engendered in persons from other counties resulted in branches being formed elsewhere. In Dublin pioneers of the movement were Rev. Dr Yore, St Paul's, Arran Quay and Rev. Dr Spratt of the Carmelite Friars, Whitefriar St. Limerick was also prominent in this and when Fr Theobald visited that city to preach a charity sermon in aid of the Presentation Sisters' school, on his arrival by train the night before (13 November 1839) the streets were filled with crowds from the country. Standing-room in a cellar for sleeping accomodation was priced at two shillings. The bishop desired the friar to administer the pledge the day following the charity sermon and while doing so from the front steps of the home of Mr Dunbar, his brother-in-law, in Upper Mallow St, the crowd surging forward broke down the railing. To prevent people being crushed to death at the next venue in front of the court-house, a troop of the Royal Scots Greys and the Black Watch were called in to control the crowd. That day he en-rolled more than 150,000 persons. Towards the end, his voice having failed, he called to his assistance some priests who were present.

Apart from that visit to Limerick, which had not been connected with his anti-drink campaign, and another soon after requested by the Bishop of Waterford, Fr Mathew refused invitations to other places as he had received ecc-lesiastic approval only in Cork. As time advanced bishops and clergy forgot their scepticism and the friar was inundated with formal requests to preach and administer the pledge in their dioceses. During 1840 he was seldom in Cork, so he appointed three (later increased to four) friars to carry out Capuchin duties in the city.

THE 'CROTTYITES' OF BIRR

Early in the New Year, 1841, he visited the chief towns of Tipperary, then on to Ennis and Birr in which latter town the Resident Magistrate fearing that the police would not be sufficent to control the crowd had obtained a troop of Lancers from Athlone. This unusual precaution was due to a dire state of affairs which existed in the town for more than twenty years, following the suspension, by the bishop, of the parish priest, Fr Crotty. This disgruntled clergyman left the Church and started a rival religious body to which the majority of the inhabitants flocked and where their former pastor preached the doctrine of 'nothing is to be feared but Popery'.

The parishioners, considering that their pastor had been persecuted, carried out a campaign of hatred against anyone in clerical garb and refrained from walking on the same side of the street as a priest. As far back as 1826 Dr Doyle, Bishop of Kildare and Leighlin, had come at the invitation of the local bishop to try to bring peace between the latter and the recalcitrant 'Crottyites', but he failed completely.

The one hope lay in the intervention of the popular Fr Mathew who, on his requested visit in 1840, preached a memorable sermon on peace and mercy which had a good response but was soon forgotten after his departure. Deciding that the only solution lay in the gentle influence of nuns to counteract the rough rebellious nature which defied the authority of bishop and priests, and having gained permission, Fr Mathew now approached his friend, Mother Catherine McAuley, requesting her to make a Sister of Mercy foundation in the town. For this he could promise her no foundation fund but that her 'inducement must be the conversion of the incorrigibles'. To this he added: 'Give me for Birr truly spiritual persons — souls that rely entirely on God's providence'.

The one suitable leader of Mother McAuley's select group of nuns was unfortunately suffering from the old dreaded 'consumption', but soon her condition improved remarkably; this was followed by equally remarkable results when she and those in her charge took up duty in the new convent. Their influence on the children in their new school and on the adults whom they visited in their homes was immediate. Shortly afterwards there took place the ceremony of 'clothing' of two postulants in the parish church at which the bishop officiated and Fr Mathew preached. Following this a return to the fold proceeded rapidly. When the foundress — Mother Aloysius Scott — died in 1844 there was not a single schismatic in the district and a few years later Fr Crotty came back to the Church, a heart-broken, repentant man. The recovery of Mother Aloysius for the telling few years was held by Mother McAuley as being wholly due to Fr Mathew's prayers.

In March 1841 Fr Mathew reached Galway where for the first time he met Daniel O'Connell. O'Connell was deeply impressed by the influence the friar had aroused, and wondered if he could enlist such a power in the Repeal Campaign. This hope could never be realized as Fr Mathew was adamant that no hint of politics could be attributed to the Total Abstinence Movement. In this decision he went to the extreme of not casting his vote in elections. The wearing of temperance badges or the attendance of temperance bands to play at political meetings was strictly forbidden by him.

On Saturday 28 March 1841 he arrived in Dublin and next day preached in the Pro-Cathedral, Marlborough St, where 6,000 people were present including the Hon. Mr Fortescue, son of the Lord Lieutenant. Next morning he addressed a huge open air meeting at the rere of the Custom House. On the platform were Rev. Dr Yore and other prominent clergy; also Fr Theobald's old schoolboy friend, Charles Bianconi, now a wealthy businessman and pioneer of road transport. Some students of Trinity College made the friar a guest of honour at a temperance tea-party. To nine of them he presented a silver medal after administering the pledge to them and in recognition of the example that their 'station and talent would afford'.

A special meeting he arranged for women in the Royal Exchange when they complained of not having been able to get near for the pledge through the crowd of men at the meeting. He made three further visits to Dublin that year.

In June 1841 he preached at the consecration of the new parish church in Maynooth after which he was brought by the President of the College to address the students and some honoured guests: eight professors and 250 students were enrolled as members. How his mind must have gone back to that illicit party which he had given, and his subsequent ignominious departure! He remained for a few days as a guest of the Duke of Leinster at Carton House but there was never a hope of relaxation as crowds demanded his attention; 35,000 pledges were given out before he left.

In Athy, the mail-coach in which he was travelling was

held up for five hours by a milling crowd, after which a protest at the 'Stopping of Her Majesty's Mail' appeared in an English newspaper. Contrary to expectations, a letter to Fr Mathew sent by Purcell, proprietor of the mail service, was not a reproach but a request that he should make free use of the coaches 'to further the holy cause of temperance'. Bianconi about the same time placed his public transport at the friar's disposal.

Reference to individual places where Fr Mathew conducted his campaign could become tedious but Ulster claims a mention. The Repeal Movement had aroused bitter feelings among Orangemen, so well-wishers tried to dissuade the priest from going there but, as he told the first meeting in Newry in August 1841, he had 'too much reliance on the honour of Irishmen to suppose the people of this province would arise in their might and crush one humble individual who was merely trying to promote public morality'. He also let them know of his disapproval of the suggestion of superstition which arose from the attendance at meetings of physically afflicted people who believed that he had curative powers. While on that Northern tour Fr Mathew could not accept an invitation to visit Belfast and Lisburn as the Catholic bishop of Down and Connor was not sympathetic to the total abstinence crusade. To meet the wishes of the people there, a meeting was arranged in Moira, Co. Down, outside that diocese, and later at Warrenpoint, where at a subsequent banquet Gavan Duffy exhorted Fr Mathew to establish lecture- and reading-rooms and such facilities in the society's branches. So impressed was the friar with this speech that he had 30,000 copies printed and circulated.

It was not only the poor and middle strata of Irish society but officialdom as well which was loud in its praise of the results of the temperance campaign. In the House of Lords complimentary references were made by Lord Ebrington, the Marquis of Normanby (a former Viceroy of Ireland), the Earl of Devon and the Earl of Wicklow: which sentiment was echoed by Irish landlords — the Duke of Devonshire, the Marquis of Lansdowne, Lord John Russell and Lord Morpeth, the Irish Chief Secretary. The latter declared, 'the duty of the police and military in Ireland is now almost entirely confined to keeping the ground clear for the operations of Fr Mathew'.

In a letter, Maria Edgeworth wrote in 1840 to the secretary of the Irish Temperance Union, referring to the remarkable improvement which the extensive taking of the pledge had brought about in her village, Edgeworthtown. A quotation from it shows a most important achievement in the battle against excessive drinking, especially in Ireland where drunkenness was — and unfortunately still is — regarded as a joke. Her remarks run thus: 'Very few, scarcely any instances of breaking the pledge have yet come to our knowledge; but some have occurred. The culprits have been completely shunned and disgraced so that they are awful warnings to others. I consider Fr Mathew as the greatest benefactor to his country, the most true friend to Irishmen and to Ireland'. Contrary sentiments were no doubt held by the Chancellor of the Exchequer at the fall of revenue from Irish spirit duty of £1,434,573 in 1839 to £852,418 in 1844.

A grand procession of the Total Abstinence Society held in Cork on Easter Monday 1842 was attended by Daniel O'Connell as Lord Mayor of Cork, which latter presence caused Fr Mathew a little uneasiness in case it might give the impression of co-operation between the Repeal and the Temperance movement. Again he strongly resisted all efforts of O'Connell in this regard. The Liberator's high opinion of the friar is summed up in his declaration that he was 'the most useful man Ireland had ever produced'.

Dublin was not to be left behind in its display of appreciation of the work of the friar and a public meeting was arranged to take place in the Theatre Royal. The public annoucement was signed by 'four Catholic bishops, two dukes, four marquises, nineteen earls, ten viscounts and barons, upwards of forty baronets and thirty members of parliament', as was pointed out by the secretary; the Duke of Leinster presided.

In trying to whittle down the number of tributes it would be difficult to exclude that of a New York puritan, Mrs Asenath Nicholson, who visited Ireland in 1844 to investigate the condition of the poor and their religious beliefs. Greatly impressed by what she learned at first hand by seeking her nightly lodgings in the cottages as she travelled along, she recorded all in a diary. A few telling words sum up her impression of Fr. Mathew. She wrote: 'I must acknowledge that he is the only person of whom I had heard much praise who ever exceeded the expectation given'. Her ending words have become almost traditional: 'He has wiped more tears from the face of women than any other being on the globe but the Lord Jesus'.

Thackeray in his *Irish Sketch Book* describes a meeting with Fr Mathew: 'With whose face a thousand little print-shop windows had already rendered me familiar . . . He is a stout, handsome, honest-looking man, exceeding simple, hearty and manly — about the only man that I have met in Ireland who in speaking of public affairs does not talk as a partisan . . . avoiding all political questions, no man seems more eager than he for the practical improvement of this country. Leases and rents, farming implements, reading societies, music societies: he was full of these and of his schemes of temperance above all'

A fitting ending to tributes paid to the Great Crusader's success was conveyed in a letter to him in 1841 from Rev. Dr Paul Cullen, Rector of the Irish College in Rome, who stated that the Pope (Gregory XVI) had spoken most favourably of his achievements and had made a suggestion of conferring some honour on him in appreciation. There is no record of such having been received however.

CRITICISM

Let us now turn from praiseworthy tributes and face the inevitable adverse criticism which achivement in any field arouses. From the beginning there had been arguments that the success of its leader's ideal was impossible; that his place was in the seclusion of his friary and not in the public market-place. Far greater hurt was given by the attitude of some of his fellow clergy who held that in his relationship with Protestants he had taken an unduly liberal attitude. Most distressing of all was the censure of the Archbishop of Tuam, John MacHale, who held the view that a pledge for five years would be sufficient. He was also loud in his criticism of the Total Abstinence Movement in general but of its leader in particular for his practice of going from diocese to diocese addressing meetings. He launched a public and personal attack on the latter, whom he termed 'a vagabond friar', and also on his sincerity which he termed 'the mercantile manipulation of the Total Abstinence Society'. He also passed some deprecating comments on the sale of medals. Fr Mathew made no reply but in a letter to Dr

Cullen in Rome may be seen his speculation as to the reason of his not having received the promised papal sign of appreciation: 'I am well aware of the quarter whence these accusations against me have been sent to Rome but I prefer to suffer in silence rather than afford the enemies of the Catholic Church a cause for triumph by vindicating myself'.

There was further opposition from a small body of extreme Protestants who declared the Total Abstinence Crusade to be a disguised campaign against the religion of the Gospel — 'a sort of Trojan horse which some of these nights will sally forth on the sleeping sentinels of Ireland and make it an easy prey'. An application by Fr Mathew to hold a meeting on the Rock of Cashel was refused by the Rector with the statement that 'Temperance was of the devil'. A Protestant clergyman in Derry wrote in the *Morning Chronicle* that pledge-giving was 'highly insulting to the majesty of God'; while some Orange farmers at Loughall, Co. Armagh, refused to employ labourers who had taken the pledge.

VISITS TO SCOTLAND AND ENGLAND

The thought of the many Irish people in English and Scottish cities influenced Fr Mathew finally to accept the many invitations to visit there and so, accompanied by his secretary McKenna, he arrived in August 1842 at Glasgow. There they started on a round of temperance meetings in all of which he received great enthusiasm as in Ireland. On leaving, he decided to return to Cork via Belfast, the only large town in Ireland where he had never addressed the people, as the Bishop of Down and Connor had not given permission. As from 1 August 1841 the Pope had conferred on the friar the title of Commissary Apostolic of the Province (Ireland) which meant that he was deputy of the Holy See and was directly subject to its authority and to none other. (This, however, was not the honour previously intended.) On leaving the ship he thanked the cheering crowd and hesitated about acquiescing to their demand for the pledge, but the arrival of his train from Lurgan saved him from further embarrassment.

Shortly after his arrival in Cork he went for his annual holiday to his old home, Rathclogheen, and there enjoyed a family reunion of two generations. His own, the older set, were not all as enthusiastic as he was about the object of his missionary zeal, especially his brother John, now the head of the house. John was an upholder of the excellence of whiskey punch — though not to an excessive degree — and he had to curb his appetite in that direction, much to the amusement of the Apostle who remembered his own appreciation of that particular beverage before self-sacrifice and the necessity of good example caused him to abjure 'the flowing bowl'.

In the summer of 1843 Fr Mathew was overcome at the death of his brother Frank in his home Rockview, Co. Tipperary, aged only 42 years. The priest grieved at the thought of the young widow, left with ten fatherless children, but with work awaiting him he returned to Cork with his brother Charles after the burial in the family grave in Thomastown.

The following month he set out to fulfill a promised visit to England, starting with Liverpool where the people were living in great poverty; from there to Yorkshire and Manchester where, incidentally, for the first time he gave the pledge both in English and in simple Irish language. Thomas Carlyle, who happened to be passing one of these meetings, asked his hackney driver to stop and afterwards described the speaker to his wife as 'a broad, solid-looking man with grey hair, mild intelligent eyes, rather aquiline nose and countenance. The very face of him attracts you. I almost cried to listen to him and could not but lift my broad-brim at the end when he called for God's blessing on the vow these poor wretches had taken'.

London was his next mission-field and there the upper ranks of society welcomed him. To quote from an account: 'He was the lion of the season and was overwhelmed with invitations. People wondered to find that the Irish friar was quite a civilized being, calm and pleasant and not in the least dazzled by the most brilliant of receptions; "quite like one of ourselves".' His chief objective, however, was the poverty-stricken inhabitants of Westminster, the East end and all London slums. His innate courtesy, on the other hand, caused him to comply with established mode of action in calling on personages who had sent him invitations and thereby he won for his cause several persons of distinction.

Lists of those who sought his presence include the Marchioness of Wellesley; several ladies of the Queen's household;

the Earl of Arundel, eldest son of the Duke of Norfolk; the Earl of Clanricarde, to mention but a few. A distinguished Jesuit, Rev. J. Conmee, addressing a large audience stated that 'the great Capuchin occupied an acknowledged position in the history of the British Empire. As proof of this he mentioned how the National Portrait Gallery of Historical Celebrities, then recently created in London, had placed his portrait high among the worthies of sixty years since'.

However, all was not a triumphal march for the Apostle, especially in London where there were several disturbing incidents such as an organised and successful effort by worshippers of the bottle to break up a meeting at Blackheath; this was later greatly criticized by the press. Recurrences at Greenwich and Westminster were met by the priest with a calm attitude and quick Irish repartee which gained praise for him and discomfort for his adversaries. Such was the case with a man who, trying to stir up the crowd, cried out, 'What good can come to you from that man? He is only a popish monk', to which Fr Theobald retorted, 'Have you not received Christianity from a popish monk?, the Reformation from a popish monk — Martin Luther?' Were it not for police intervention he would sometimes have met with personal violence.

Cambridge to which he was invited was his next venue, but on arrival the use of the Town Hall was refused. An avalanche of opposition followed in sermons preached, handbills and posters distributed. In one such, Fr Mathew was described as 'a priest of an idolatrous Church and a worshipper of the wafer God'. Despite all this, many clergy of the Established Church and some Dissenting ministers were present at a meeting in St Andrew's Hall.

Following the priest's return home, to honour the achievement of his English mission William O'Connor, a Cork merchant tailor, had a monument erected at personal expense in the grounds of Mount Patrick, overlooking the Lee at Glanmire. The foundation stone was laid in 1843 and it was erected in 1845 and became known as the Mathew Tower. An article in the *Irish Times,* 24 July 1980, throws a modern light on this memorial. It stated how, a short time before, a Belfast man, while digging in his garden, had unearthed 'a large metal plaque which had at some stage been fixed to Fr Mathew's Folly near Dunkettle outside Cork city.' The newspaper article speculated that as the tower had been erected in private grounds no one had responsibility for its upkeep and so 'weather and local vandals had left it in a sorry condition of dereliction'. It was reported that a Dublin development company had acquired it, with purpose unknown. The Ulster museum had decided to return the plaque to Cork.

Another likeness of Fr Mathew was mentioned in a letter to himself from Fr Francis Mahony (the Fr Prout of 'The Bells of Shandon' renown). In describing a visit which he made to the General of the Capuchins in Rome, he wrote how he had ordered a bust to be sculpted by Hogan depicting the 'Irish Capuchin robed in the cowl and habit of his order', and how he had later seen it in the Barberini Convent with its inscription 'Frater Theobaldus Mathew', underneath which was given a summary of his country of origin and of his mission. Now in the Capuchin Friary in Church St, Dublin, it is described in detail in John Turpin's recent book, *John Hogan* (catalogue no. 41).

FINANCIAL DIFFICULTIES

About that time, while at a meeting in the North Monastery Christian Brothers' School in Cork, where 2,500 people received the pledge, when replying to the speech of thanks Fr Mathew astounded those present by suddenly declaring in a sad tone, 'Though your excellent chairman has wished me the enjoyment of many happy days I must say I enjoy very few moments of happiness. My very heart is eaten up by care and solicitude of every kind'. Almost immediately, however, he regained his customary peaceful attitude. In time to come the cause of this anguish of soul was to become known.

From the start Fr Mathew considered that a token of membership in the form of a medal and card should be given without charge to takers of the pledge, and this continued until 1843, when the secretary, McKenna, discovered that the society was £5,000 in debt.

It was with great reluctance that the Leader agreed to a price of one shilling being requested but finally even that did not improve matters as many, many thousands were given free (some to specified groups such as soldiers, sailors, emigrants and schools of children), which loss was added to by lavishness and lack of business acumen. An example of the latter was the return some years later, when the financial bubble had burst, of 1,400 ordinary burnished pewter and white metal medals and twenty silver ones, which had been ordered but for which distributions and payment was never made. One in gold Fr Mathew presented as a token of gratitude to a Mrs O'Reilly, Co. Cavan, in whose house he had stayed, and to each member of the family he gave a silver one. Another similar mark of appreciation in gold was referred to by the noted numismatist, Dr A.J. Went, in a paper read to the Old Dublin Society in 1977; this medal which had been presented to the Rev. Dr John Miley — as was inscribed on the edge — 'weighs 1·88 fine ounces, the bullion value of which in the 1840's would have been about £8, a considerable sum in those days. During the Maynooth visit in 1840, £200 worth of medals were distributed and on these, as on all silver tokens, no charge was made. A year following his visit to Scotland in 1842, a gold chalice was delivered to the Church of St Mary's, Glasgow, and inscribed thus 'Presented to the Right Rev. Dr Murdoch by the Very Rev. Theobald Mathew, Commissary Apostolic, Glasgow August 1843'.

The truth is that Fr Mathew was neither improvident nor careless about incurring debts, except in relation to his mission. Regarding personal debt he never owed a shilling, denying himself even of necessities until he had enough money to pay for them. Large extra sums of money were required in connection with the Holy Trinity Church building in Cork, the collection for which had to be abandoned on account of the famine. His brother Charles had now a large family so his constant help in the past could not be called upon.

Medals were not the only expenditure: provision of band instruments and printed matter also caused an excessive drain, as did large donations to societies and institutions connected with his missionary activities, following out his favourite maxim 'Give, give, give'.

The greatest trial was the freely circulated rumour that he was making money for himself and his family. One prominent newspaper argued that if he had given the pledge to four million people he must have sold that number of medals, for which he would have received £200,000. When he was £7,000 in debt and to quote his biographer, Rogers, 'his relatives had been reduced almost to poverty', it was publicly stated that he had enriched both himself and them at the expense of society. Earlier in his campaign a member of his family connected to him by marriage had written, 'My immediate family has been absolutely and totally ruined by Fr Mathew's temperance movement'.

At the start of his crusade he had been accustomed to broadcasting largesse, having in mind the prospect of a large legacy which his god-mother, Lady Elizabeth, had repeatedly promised him; but when she died suddenly on 14 December 1841 it was discovered that she had made him one of her executors but had left him nothing. It was said that she would have bequeathed him (who apart from being her god-son was her favourite young cousin) the Thomastown estate, but for the fact that thereby it would become the property of the Capuchin order. In expectation of the bequest he had allowed his financial situation to worsen and had drawn freely on his family's resources intending to use the bequest to meet his commitments. Even if she left nothing to Fr Mathew it seems very strange that she did not leave the property to one of his brothers, of the Mathew name — sons of her cousin James, with which family she was on friendly terms; her three brothers had been god-parents to some of them. It will be remembered that earlier it was stated that she left the property to Viscount Rohan de Chapot, a French cousin on her mother's side, and that he gave large house-parties in Thomastown. Possibly she may have been anxious that the castle's former pattern of lavish entertainment should live on, as would not have been possible with the depleted fortune of the Mathew family and also the deterrent of their Catholic background.

Matters came to a head in a dramatic manner soon after the friar returned from the English mission. In August 1844, while giving the pledge in Chapelizod during his Dublin visit, a bailiff engaged by a Birmingham firm of medal manufacturers took the opportunity of kneeling with the crowd to ask for a blessing; having received it, he rose and quietly handed the priest a writ. The latter took it and calmly continued his work of the moment.

His family had borne the brunt of his reckless benevolence, so he could not call on them to stem the flood-tide. Two of his brothers who were large capital holders of distilleries in Cashel and Midleton had suffered great loss in their efforts to help him and had to relinquish their distillery interest and take up agriculture.

The news of his arrest electrified his admirers into action and meetings were called to raise funds. In some cases the loudest proclaimed brought minimum results, as evidenced in a newspaper report of one in the Theatre Royal. It stated that 'not one twentieth of the grand folk who signed the requisition for the meeting paid a farthing'. Others, however, gave generously, and finally, in England, an influential committee was formed. It consisted of 'the Marquis of Lansdowne, Lord John Russell, Sir Robert Peel and many other of high social rank, of both religions and of various shades of politics'; the Earl of Arundel and Surrey was President. An appeal was made for immediate relief of the Capuchin friar's pressing need and for a fund which would provide him with an annuity for life. Seven thousand pounds was the amount agreed on, which would have given him £500 a year. Subscriptions did come in but the project did not develop as the tragic famine of 1847 intervened. A Civil List pension was then suggested by Lord John Russell, the Prime Minister, and others, but Queen Victoria considered 'the one to Fr Mathew a doubtful proceeding. It is quite true that he has done much by preaching temperance but by the aid of superstition, which can hardly be patronised by the Crown'. Not knowing of this refusal, Fr Mathew, in a letter two days later to a friend, had written: 'As I feared it would injure the cause to have me paid by the government, I gratefully declined the kind proposal'. In June 1847, in a letter to the Prime Minister, Fr Mathew did request the grant of a pension, stating that 'there is not one pound in my purse'. His letter showed his incorrect assumption that the previous suggestion of a pension was the spontaneous act of the Queen. A reply came shortly afterwards from Lord John Russell to say that the Queen had directed that an annual pension of £300 should be settled on him. Fr Mathew never knew that considerable persuasion must have been brought to bear on Her Majesty to change her mind. This inadequate annuity only enabled Fr Mathew to take out a life insurance policy of £5,000 which he hoped would settle any debts outstanding at his death.

To the previous financial worry was soon added the burden of trying to help the poor, under the crushing blow of the famine which raised its head in the autumn of 1845. Correspondence from him to Trevelyan, Secretary of the Treasury, drew attention to a further blight which he had noted on a journey from Cork to Dublin, and later he wrote urging against the danger of the 'cornering' of food supplies, but he was ignored. This advice of his was actually counteracted by an announcement from Lord John Russell that no interference would be made with merchants, or with the retail trade, regarding the supply of foodstuffs to the country. As Fr Mathew had predicted, this resulted in a benefit to speculators, as was evident some months later when a commission reported that corn bought in Cork for £9-£10 was sold for £17.10; and in Limerick, where there was no corn, meal reached £19 a ton. In the first four months of 1847 in the city of Cork 2,130 people had died in the workhouse and hundreds more outside; 67 bodies were buried in one day.

Fr Mathew advocated a complete change in the economic and social system then prevailing in the country. He sought a change from the dependence of the poor on the potato crop for their food and on pigs for their rent, and he urged the growing of flax for which he supplied some small farmers with flax and other seed. Later, realizing that technical advice was necessary, he wrote to the Flax Cultivation Society in Belfast, requesting the personal counsel of an expert, with all expenses paid, to give advice on seven acres of flax which he had prevailed on his brother to grow near Cashel and thereby to encourage and instruct the local cottiers. To further this project he made arrangements for the apprenticeship of his nephew, Robert Mathew, with the owner of a flax mill near Strabane. None of his proposals was accepted and no encouragement came from the Belfast society.

In April of that year, 1847, when the scourge was at its height, a further trial awaited Fr Mathew when the Bishop of Cork died. Following the meeting of the Canons of the diocese to select a possible successor, three names were sent to Rome, that of Fr Mathew being first on the list; it was presumed by all that he would be chosen. Consternation came later when such was found to be not the case. It transpired that the Archbishop of Cashel had influenced the Pope's selection in overruling the Canons' suggestion. It was thought that this was done on account of the friar's financial embarrassments. The decision naturally disappointed Fr Mathew, although he felt relief at having been spared the responsibility which would have interfered with his missionary work. He was, however, upset at the thought that the people might take his rejection as a sign of the Holy See's disapproval of his temperance crusade.

The effects of the famine in listlessness and despair had left their mark on the populace, as was shown at the meetings in the falling off of numbers due to death, emigration and evictions which followed. In 1849 over 278,000 persons had fled from misery to Liverpool. Further despondence had come with the news of the death of O'Connell in faraway Genoa and the temptation to drown all sorrow with alcohol gradually gained ground and added great distress to the temperance advocate.

Although Fr Mathew strictly adhered to his non-interference attitude towards politics, his sympathy went out to the Young Irelanders after their arrest in 1848 and especially to his friend Gavan Duffy, who was imprisoned for more than seven months without trial. At his subsequent trial the friar testified that he was 'a man of the highest integrity and principle'. In spite of this action of his there was criticism of the friar from members who advocated revolutionary methods which he condemned.

ILLNESS; THE AMERICAN MISSION

In April 1848 there was widespread dismay at the news that Fr Mathew had been stricken by paralysis which occurred towards the end of his rigorous Lenten fast. It did not come altogether as a surprise to his friends who had been urging him to ease off his inordinate amount of work; meetings of long duration and in all weathers; constant attendance on victims of the famine; long land and sea journeys; duties connected with his position as Provincial of the Capuchin Order; and — most detrimental of all to health — his financial worries and unwarranted critical opposition. General relief was felt when it soon became known that the use of his limbs returned, but his brisk alertness and his bright appearance

[41]

had gone. After two months' convalescence in Cork he insisted on a visit to the Total Abstinence Societies in Dublin which, due to the efforts of Fr Spratt and others, had survived better than elsewhere.

Back in Cork he set to work at reorganising the societies there, many of which had lost their office leaders through the famine and thereby their general membership. In the New Year, however, he caused astonishment by announcing that he was about to set out for a missionary tour of America. He had in mind the vast number of exiles who had fled there from the famine and realized the difficulties and loneliness which would have beset them in trying to find a foot-hold in a strange land, with the danger of their seeking solace in strong drink.

His physician, Dr O'Connor, gives a description of the havoc that his illness had wrought on him, saying it was as 'though a cloud had passed over his mind and he was no longer the brilliant advocate of temperance. His gait was every day more enfeebled, and intellectual labour became a struggle; still he worked with more ardour than at any time previous, as if he were the more anxious to utilize a life which he felt was now drawing to a close'.

Persisting with his plan to extend his mission to America, he arrived on Staten Island on 1 July 1849, attended by his secretary, David O'Meara, successor to McKenna, who had died three years before. The ships of all nations at anchor in the harbour hung out their ensigns in greeting and the cheering was deafening. The following two weeks he spent in New York, attending levees and a special banquet in the City Hall, in addition to his missionary work. After a few weeks he left for Boston to be received by the Mayor and with his usual success he enrolled '45,000 and upwards since his arrival'. There arose a bitter opposition, however, from a party which coupled their temperance advocacy with that of abolition of slavery. Fr Mathew had turned down an invitation to attend a latter meeting as he feared by doing so he would arouse the animosity of a large section of the people against his temperance campaign.

On his return to New York he became seriously ill with profuse bleeding. Realizing his condition, he drew up a document stating himself to be of sound mind and had it signed by his secretaries. In it he referred no less than four times to his 'beloved brother Charles', as later recorded in

O'Meara's diary, requesting him among other things 'to take charge of the education of the three youngest children of his dead brother Francis, these being John, Robert and Victoria.

In spite of his illness, a week or so later he left for Philadelphia to carry on his usual morning-to-night round of lecturing and pledge-giving. He proceeded from there to Washington, where he was elected to a seat in the Bar of the United States Senate, an honour only once before bestowed on a foreigner, that being the Marquis de Lafayette.

In almost two years, from December 1849 to November 1851, he had traversed America from the Atlantic seaboard to the Mississippi. In New Orleans he had his most laborious and successful mission, in less than two weeks having pledged 6,000 persons. In Little Rock he was asked to remain permanently. In all places he made his customary lavish distribution of medals without charge, so again financial difficulty raised its head. His health was still precarious, resulting in tremulous limbs, and at times his mind seriously depressed, so a change was made to Pensacola, Florida, where he celebrated Mass at the Naval dockyard with over 600 persons present. On the day before the thirteenth anniversary of his setting up of the Total Abstinence Crusade he became very ill while on the journey from New Orleans to Nashville; his life being in danger he decided to return to Ireland. In his tour of America he had visited twenty five states, had addressed meetings in over 300 cities and towns, and had given the pledge to 600,000 people. On 8 November 1851 he started for Ireland where on Sunday, 6 December 1851, a group of well wishers, including his brother Charles, awaited his arrival. When he stepped from the train there was a gasp of surprise at the appearance of his grey hair, pale, drawn face and feeble gait. Too weak to address the crowd he departed with Charles for Lehenagh.

CURES ATTRIBUTED TO FR MATHEW

Refreshed after a night's rest he drove to Cork next day and visited the Temperance reading rooms, where he addressed well-wishers. He was relieved of his duties as Provincial and he resigned his superiorship of the Presentation and Ursuline Convents. He was persuaded by Dr O'Connor to give up —

even temporarily — his guidance of the Temperance Movement, which had now greatly fallen off. The next three years he stayed at Lehenagh House with his brother Charles. There his infirmities often prevented him from saying Mass, in which case he arose at 5 a.m. as usual and spent hours in meditation and prayer before joining the family at breakfast. His brother could not prevent the steady flow of people, to seek help, some being reluctantly brought along by distressed relations.

It may come as a surprise to present-day Irish people, that a good number of cures — bodily and mental — were attributed to Fr Mathew. In Fr Augustine's *Footsteps of Fr Mathew* several are quoted, but of course with the reservation that Rome is the only real arbitrator on the authenticity of such claims. One of these events was reported in two local newspapers which stated that during Fr Mathew's passage through Limerick in January 1842 a man who had broken his pledge on Christmas Eve, after which he suffered a severe stroke, was carried from the hospital to Moore's Hotel, where Fr Mathew was staying. The priest administered the pledge again, in a kindly manner and the man instantly rose up and walked to his home. 'Without delay he resumed his active and vigorous employment in the Butter Weigh House'.

Another account is given of a young lady of position and intelligence whose suffering from severe headaches was not alleviated by medical treatment. One day the violence was so great that she went to Lehenagh House, where the friar was invalided, and there implored him to cure her. He replied that 'the power to cure rests with God alone. I have no such power'. To her further entreaty of 'Then bless me and pray for me. Place your hand on my head', he did so and the lady returned home perfectly cured; there was no recurrence. The question remains, of course, could not the result be due to the power of imagination or of mind over matter?

A further incident which dealt with affliction of the mind again took place in Lehenagh House. A young man was being brought to Cork Mental Asylum 'bound on a car with his limbs tied with cords and his head exposed to the rays of a fierce sun'. On the way a suggestion was made that the invalid should first be carried to Lehenagh House. There Fr Theobald, filled with pity, requested the loosening of the cords and to have a cover put on the man's head. His calm, soothing voice had a wonderful effect on the sufferer who shortly before he had a violent paroxysm. With confidence in Fr Mathew he became calm and said that if he were brought home he would do everything asked of him. At the priest's intercession this was done and in a month's time as 'a handsome young man, well-dressed and well-mannered, he came to Lehenagh to return the priest thanks for what he had done for him'.

In the early summer of 1943 Fr Augustine, the author of the book quoted above, visited St Joseph's cemetery in Cork, where the caretaker, an intelligent and reliable man, told how people still came to pray at Fr Mathew's grave and that he had been told of several favours received. One such he said had occurred in August 1933 and is of particular interest. It was connected with a man of seventy years who had completely lost his sight following an accident in California. The doctors having given him no hope of a cure, he decided to seek the aid of one to whose memory he had deep devotion since childhood in his native Cork where his mother used to bring him to pray at the grave of Fr Mathew. After his arrival back in his native city, he went with the guidance of a helper every Monday and Friday to the grave and having prayed he began to find relief, first seeing shadows, then flashes of light and blurred objects until finally he was able to go there unassisted. On New Year's Day, four months later, he returned to his family in California, his sight perfectly restored. A final example is given in the author's words of a 'very remarkable case of a cure of a diseased bone which cure was stated to have been obtained through Fr Mathew's intercession, but this one having been sent to Rome for examination we refrain from dealing with it here'. One wonders what resulted from that examination?

Recently there was an announcement of the canonization in Rome of a foreign Capuchin friar. Perusing the lives of papal-adjudged saints of modern times, one is tempted to compare their claims with those of our Irish Fr Mathew. His sanctity, humility, selflessness, veritable martyrdom of physical and mental suffering were outstanding, added to all of which was his widespread achievement against evil in Western Europe and throughout America. Why have these traits not received similar acknowledgement? Possibly the fault lies with ourselves in not having been interested enough to persistently present his cause to Rome.

In the Autumn of 1853, in spite of his serious condition of health, the resolute friar ventured to Limerick where he gave the pledge to a large number. This probably was his last appearance at a public meeting. In October 1854, on medical advice, for the benefit of a warm climate he went to Madeira but he made no progress there as reports kept coming in of the deterioration of the temperance movement. The following August he returned to Ireland but an attempt to resume duties in the Cork Friary told on his reserve of strength and he was brought to the home of his brother completely broken down. Increased suffering and the fear of burdening the household with his final illness made him insist on removing to Cobh, to a house run by a faithful follower, John Sullivan at 18, The Beach, on the sea front. One morning in November 1855 he went down with a stroke which left him with only slight motion of the fingers. After he had been anointed his brother Charles, who was summoned from Lehenagh, asked, 'Theobald, would you like to be buried with Frank and Tom in Tipperary?' to which the dying man attempted to shake his head. 'Is it in the cemetery?', enquired Charles, meaning St Joseph's Cemetery, for which Fr Mathew had been responsible; by a movement of the fingers assent was indicated. After several days of unconsciousness, 'death came very peacefully on the feast of the Immaculate Conception, Monday, 8 December 1856, in the sixty-seventh year of his age, the forty-fourth of his priesthood and the fifteenth of his Apostolate'.

Thousands came to pay respect to his remains which were clothed in the Capuchin habit as it lay before the high altar in the Church of the Holy Trinity. His funeral procession took an hour and a half to pass through the closed-down, shuttered city. The Bishop of Cork recited the prayers over his grave at St Joseph's cemetery and his body was then laid to rest under the large stone cross which the friar himself had erected twenty six years before.

A few weeks after his death an enormous meeting of Cork citizens was called, with the object of perpetuating his memory. The erection of a suitable statue in a prominent position was agreed on. The subsequent death of the selected sculptor, John Hogan, caused a delay until Foley's fine image was unveiled on 10 October 1864; there, in its prominent position, it welcomes the visitor to Cork.

With the passing of the founder many people thought that the hope and future of his mission had died with him. And indeed for years that followed the Total Abstinence Society, already greatly undermined by the effects of the famine, fought a losing battle against disloyalty in its ranks. Now it was recognised that its previous success had been entirely due to its director's personality, his hard work and dedication. There was no one to come forward to take his place, and so loyalty faded away. Of the five million Irish people who had taken the pledge only some hundred thousand remained faithful. Within a decade of his death the movement appeared to be doomed. His secretary, Maguire, summed up the situation thus: 'Upon one man and one man alone rested the responsibility of one of the most remarkable movements and the support of one of the most extensive organisations of modern times. There was no central executive and no special fund whatever in connection with the crusade'.

In spite of the apparent final failure of Fr Theobald's campaign, such was not the case, for through his preaching and example he had generated a spiritual atmosphere, the effects of which were to become evident in years to follow. At the end of the nineteenth century a further drive against the excessive drinking scourge was directed with great success by Fr James Cullen, a member of the Jesuit Community in Gardiner St, Dublin. During his thanksgiving after Mass on Holy Rosary Sunday, October 1874, Fr Cullen was inspired, as he later stated, 'to imitate, however feebly, the great example of Fr Mathew in taking a pledge against stimulants of all kind'. Years later, on 27 December 1898, accompanied by four local ladies, a meeting was held at St Francis Xavier's Church in Gardiner St, during which they pledged themselves to a campaign of prayer and sacrifice in what Fr Cullen termed the Heroic Offering; thus was born the Pioneer Total Abstinence Association. In a short time hundreds of thousands of 'Pioneers' joined the group and rapidly the movement spread throughout Ireland and further afield.

Looking around our country today, especially her cities, at the problem of excessive drinking and the new phenomenon of drug addiction, one may only pray that comparable leadership will emerge to wrestle with these problems which effect even young people, who will shape the Ireland of tomorrow.

Salvatore Canals
JESUS AS FRIEND
Quiet thoughts about what it means
to be a Christian

Benedict Baur
FREQUENT CONFESSION
A classic book about making the best
use of this sacrament

Georges Huber
MY ANGEL WILL GO BEFORE YOU
All about the guardian angels

Federico Suarez
THE NARROW GATE
On passages of the Gospel of Saint John

Peter Rohrbach
CONVERSATION WITH CHRIST
An outline of St Teresa's teaching
about prayer

Please write for our Catalogue of books on religious subjects.

FOUR COURTS PRESS
Kill Lane, Blackrock, County Dublin